Cool Clay

By Ruby Shumaker

Mud Puddle Books

NEW YORK

Hand model: Madison Hogge
Printed in China

Table of Contents

Introduction

Kinds of Clay

There are many different kinds of clay that can be used for modeling. Each has advantages and disadvantages, depending on what it is that you want to make from the clay that you are using.

Modeling Clay:

♥ Modeling clay is nontoxic and safe for all ages to use.

♥ It will not harden, even if left unprotected. This means it can be used over and over again.

♥ This clay cannot be used for permanent creations, because it will remain soft. For example, you cannot make jewelry that you want to wear from modeling clay.

♥ It is best to make small objects from modeling clay, because it is very heavy and will not hold its shape for larger items.

♥ Modeling clay can usually be found in the kid's craft section of your local craft or hobby store.

NOTE: Some of the modeling clay found in the kid's craft section is Play Dough®. It is made from a softer compound and is more difficult to mold into smaller shapes than modeling clay. It is, however, easier for younger children to use.

Clay Dough:

♥ Made at home from cooking ingredients, clay dough is nontoxic and safe for all ages to use.

♥ Although softer than modeling clay, clay dough can also be used over and over again.

♥ Clay dough can be hardened in the oven like polymer clay.

♥ Store in an airtight container in the refrigerator to prevent drying and cracking.

Polymer Clay:

♥ Polymer clay is nontoxic and safe for all ages to use.

♥ Polymer clay should be soft when purchased. If you pur-chase clay that is too hard to knead, there are clay softeners available at your local craft store.

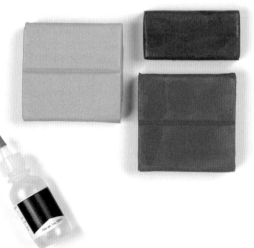

- This clay does not dry out while you are working with it, so you don't need to hurry to make a project from it.

- Bake polymer clay in the oven to create permanent projects. It will not shrink or change size but some of the clays will change color after being baked.

color before baked   color after baked

- Polymer clay should not be used to make food containers or to hold items that burn, such as candles or incense.

Working with Clays

Modeling Clay:

- Wash your hands before working with modeling clay, and between working with different colors.

- Work on a flat, clean, dry surface that is covered with a plastic sheet or disposable vinyl tablecloth.

- Knead clay before molding to soften.

- When creating a project, try working with the lighter colors first, then moving on to darker colors. This will help prevent colors from smearing onto other clays.

- If the clay sticks to your modeling tools, carefully remove as much clay as you can with a toothpick or butter knife. Clean utensils with a small scrub brush or toothbrush (one used only for clay) and warm, soapy water.

♥ Store clay in airtight containers or plastic bags that have all the air squished out.

Clay Dough:

♥ All of the instructions under Modeling Clay apply to clay dough.

♥ Most clay dough will dry out during use, so additional water may be needed to prevent cracking.

♥ Some types of clay dough can be eaten! These types of clay are used for decorating cookies, cakes, and cupcakes. Be sure to wash your hands when working with different colors to prevent mixing. Store edible clay dough in the refrigerator and clean up with warm, soapy water.

Polymer Clays:

♥ All of the instructions under Modeling Clay apply to polymer clays.

♥ To work with polymer clay, pinch, squeeze, squish, and knead as much clay as you need until it is soft enough to roll into a snake. Fold the snake over on itself a few times, roll into a snake again, and fold. Try not to get any air bubbles into the clay. Fold and roll until the ends of the clay stretch instead of break when you pull the ends.

♥ Polymer clay will stay soft until you bake it in the oven. Always follow the manufacturer's instructions for baking and always ask a grown-up to help you use the oven. NEVER put polymer clay in the microwave.

♥ You can make additions to your already-baked polymer creations by adding fresh, unbaked details and putting them back into the oven. If pieces do not stick while in the oven, use white glue to adhere them together.

General Tips:

♥ If tools are sticking to your clay, brush a little cornstarch on the clay.

♥ If polymer clay is sticking to your hands, wipe your hands with a small amount of baby oil.

♥ To remove polymer clay from your hands, use hand lotion to break down the clay. Wipe off with a paper towel, then wash with warm, soapy water.

Tools and Other Cool Stuff

You can use almost anything you want to when working with clay! Once you have used a tool for clay, it should not be used for anything else. Be sure to ask a grown-up which tools are okay for you to use. Here are some ideas:

Plastic Rolling Pin: A small rolling pin is best when trying to flatten clay evenly. Use a plastic rolling pin, not a wooden one, because the wooden one will leave marks on the clay and the clay will absorb into the wood.

A rolling pin found in the cake decorating section of your local craft or hobby store is usually a good one to use with clay. It is used for fondant* and has elastic on each end to act as a thickness guide. If your rolling pin does not have elastics, use two craft sticks on each side of the clay you are rolling to help keep the dough the same thickness.

Cutting Tools: Table knives and forks or plastic knives and forks are good for cutting and making patterns in your clay. Do not use sharp knives. You can use household items such as scissors or an egg slicer to cut your clay, or special craft

*A thick sugar and water mixture used both in the making of candy and the icing and decorating of cakes. Can be flavored and colored.

knives used with clay or rolling cutters used in fondant frosting designs.

Pattern Makers: Toothpicks and straws can be used to punch holes, or make small dots or patterns in your clay. You can also use items such as pencils, skewers, forks, paintbrushes, or whatever you can find in the drawer. Modeling tool kits made especially to work with clay or items used with fondant frosting can be purchased in your local craft store.

NOTE: Whenever using scissors, knives, or cutters ask for a grown-up's help.

Cookie Cutters or Clay Cutters: Cookie cutters come in all shapes and sizes and are an easy way to make shapes in your clay. Clay cutters are also available in the clay section of your craft and hobby store. A clay press or extruder also has many of the same shapes as a cookie cutter or clay cutter.

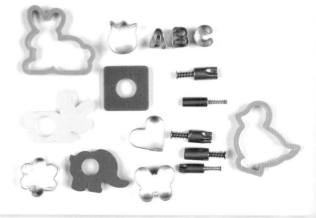

Tracing Objects: Stencils and household items can be used to trace shapes onto clay.

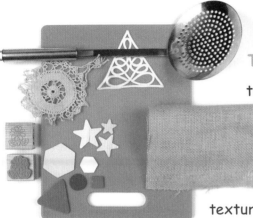

Texturing Tools: Texturing tools are whatever you want to use that will create patterns in your clay. You can use rubber stamps, textured fabric such as burlap, kitchen utensils, or wood cutouts.

Garlic Press or Clay Press: A garlic press is one of the best tools when working with clay and can be purchased in the kitchen section of most stores. A garlic press is limited to one size of clay "strings".

A clay press is similar to a garlic press; only it has a variety of inserts that can regulate the size and shape of the clay as it is squeezed through the press. This tool is often called an "extruder".

In the projects in this book you can use either a garlic press or an extruder, depending on which is best for your needs.

Neither, however, are easy objects to clean. When using a press in a project that requires many colors, do not wash

the press between colors.

1 Squeeze as much as possible of the first color clay through the press, 2 then squeeze the second color through. When the first color is finished and just a small amount of the second color appears, trim that and 3 begin the second color for the project. Continue in this manner with as many colors as are needed for the project.

Cookie Sheet: When working with polymer clay, you will want to create your projects on a cookie sheet covered in tin foil so that you can easily put them in the oven for baking.

Embellishments: When working with clay you can use anything you want to embellish your designs. Try using feathers, buttons, rhinestones, tiny paper flags or umbrellas, rubber animals, pom-poms, or whatever else your imagination can find.

Miscellaneous Items

Small Watercolor Brush: This is used to apply a small amount of water to the clay when two pieces are joined together.

Vinyl Tablecloth or Plastic Sheet: This is used to cover your work surface. It is a good idea to have a large plastic sheet as well as squares of plastic that can be used for each individual color of clay.

Tool Box: It is a good idea to have a box for storing clay and tools. This way, you will always know where they are and no one will mistake them for cooking tools! Decorate it any way you want so that everyone knows it is your clay box!

Clay Shapes

Now that you know what kinds of clay there are and what tools to use, it is time to actually make something with your clay. You may want to practice making a few shapes before you begin a project, but remember: It's only clay! If you make a mistake, you can knead the clay again and start over. And sometimes, mistakes can make the best projects of all!

Shapes

- Most projects are made from a few basic shapes. Once you master these easy shapes, you can make anything!

- These shapes are called for throughout the book in almost every project. If you do not know how to make one of the shapes refer back to these instructions.

- You will have to practice making shapes until you can guess how much clay you will need for a project. If you create your shape and it's not big enough, get more clay, knead the two pieces together, and reshape. The same is true if the piece is too large. Remove some of the clay, knead the piece again, and reshape.

- Do not make your shapes too large or too heavy. It is better to make smaller projects from the kinds of clay that are described in this book.

Ball:

1. Squish a piece of clay together with your fingers and then gently roll it into a ball between the palms of your hand.

2. Continue rolling, using even pressure with both hands until it is perfectly smooth and round.

Cone:

1. Create a ball shape following the Ball instructions.

2. Take the finished ball and pinch an end into a point.

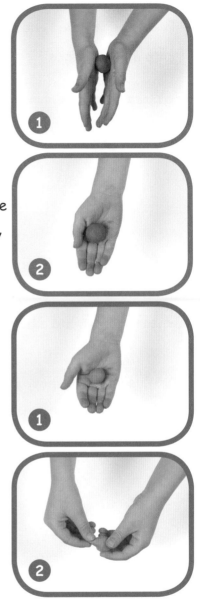

3. Roll this shape gently between your palms to keep the base round.

4. Press the rounded end of your ball onto a flat surface.

Oval:

1. Create a ball shape following the Ball instructions.

2. Now roll the ball back and forth between your hands, pressing a little more firmly than you did when rolling it into a ball.

3. Do this until the shape is longer and the ends become narrower. You now have an oval.

Sausage:

1. Create a ball shape following the Ball instructions.

2. Take the ball and roll it back and forth between the palms of your hands until it becomes longer and forms a thick sausage shape.

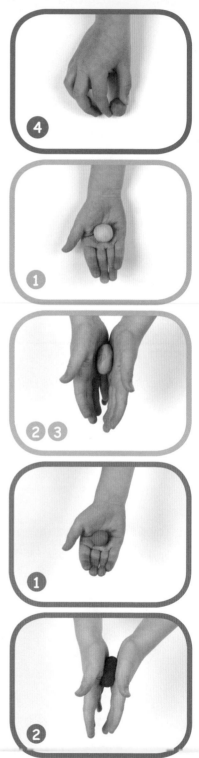

3. Next place this shape onto a tabletop and continue rolling with the palm of one hand until it is the length and the thickness that you want.

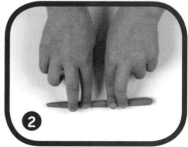

Hint: You can finish the ends by leaving them the way they are, cutting them with a knife, flattening them against the table, or pinching them off.

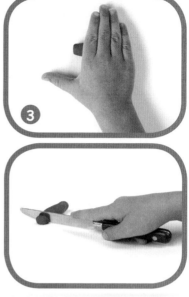

Rope:

1. Create a ball shape following the Ball instructions.

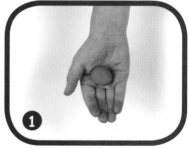

2. Lay the ball on a flat surface and use your fingers and equal pressure to roll and stretch the ball out into a rope.

3. Continue rolling and stretching until it is the length and the thickness needed for the project. It will take a little practice to get a rope that is even in thickness from end to end.

Strips:

1. Create a ball shape following the Ball instructions.

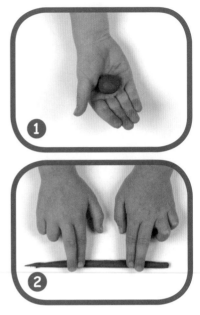

2. Create a rope shape following the Rope instructions.

3. Lay the rope on the table. If you are concerned about the thickness, lay a craft stick on either side of the rope to measure.

4. Flatten the rope with a small rolling pin. Take care to press evenly with the rolling pin and roll from the center of the rope to one end. Pick up the pin, go back to the center, and roll to the other end. Always begin in the center and roll outward, as this will help keep the strips an even thickness as well as prevent them from sticking to the rolling pin.

Cube:

1. Create a ball shape following the Ball instructions.

2. Take the ball and place it on a flat surface, then press down on the top of the ball to flatten it. Turn the ball over and repeat, until all six sides are flat. You can even the sides and smooth the corners with a flat object, such as a kitchen knife.

Slabs (square or round):

1. Create a large ball shape following the Ball instructions.

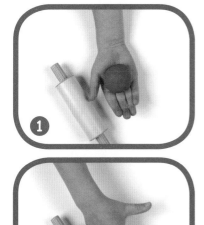

2. Lay the large ball on the table and flatten it slightly with the palm of your hand.

3. Flatten the ball with a small rolling pin following Step 4 under Strips.

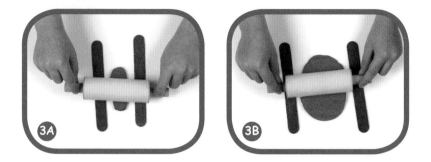

4. To make a square or round slab, cut out a square with a cookie cutter, a pattern, or use a ruler and a knife.

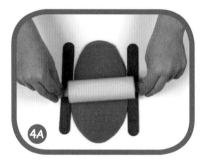

Small Circles:

1. Create a small ball shape following the Ball instructions.

2. Place the ball on a flat surface and flatten with your thumb until it is the desired shape and thickness.

Making Simple Clay Canes:

A cane is a log made from polymer clay. It is created so that you have the same design running through the entire log. Once finished, you cut slices from the log in order to have repeats of the same image. The longer you make your cane, the more slices you will have. Canes can be made in any shape—circles, triangles, squares, stars, hearts, or anything else you wish.

General Cane Tips:

♥ Use the same type and brand of clay in your cane. Baking times and consistencies vary with manufacturers.

♥ If you are making a project to keep, allow the cane to sit overnight after creating it and before cutting it. The cane becomes warm and squishy after working with it, so the pieces may be distorted when cut. A shorter way is to put the finished cane in the refrigerator for 30 minutes.

♥ Your cane should be even from one end to the other before you begin cutting but if it isn't, don't worry. The design you have created may be more to your liking than one that is perfect!

♥ Store unused canes in airtight containers when not in use. If you put the canes into plastic bags for storage the canes may be squished during storage, distorting your designs.

Marbled Cane:

1. Follow directions for making Ropes on page 17. Make as many colors of ropes as you desire.

2. Twist the ropes together.

3. Knead clay twist until desired marbling is achieved.

Hint: Do not over-knead or the colors will simply blend together into a new color.

4. Follow directions for making a Sausage on page 16. This is now your marbled cane.

5. Slice, use in project, and bake following manufacturer's directions.

Jellyroll Cane:

1. Follow directions for Slabs on page 19.

2. Make slabs in 2 or more colors and cut the same size rectangle from each.

Hint: Cut your first color slab, place on the second color, then cut around it. Repeat with each additional color.

3. Roll the slabs together into a tube.

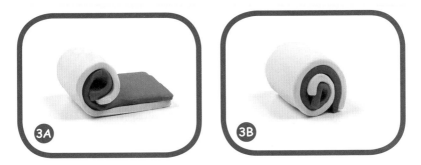

4. Slice, use in project, and bake following manufacturer's directions.

Striped Cane:

1. Follow directions for Slabs on page 19.

2. Make slabs in 2 or more colors and cut the same size rectangle from each.

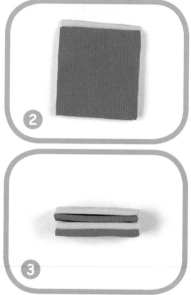

3. Cut the stack of slabs in half and repeat until you have the number of stripes that you want in your design.

4. When stack is as desired, put pressure on the stack to squish the colors together.

Hint: Be careful not to push so hard that you indent the top slab or make the slabs uneven.

5. Cut slices the thickness desired for project.

Checkerboard Cane:

1. Follow directions for making Slabs on page 19.

2. Make slabs in 2 colors and cut the same size rectangle from each.

3. Slice this slab.

4. Place slices side by side, flipping every other slice. Again gently press strips together.

5. Optional: You can now cut this slab in half and place on top of each other if you want your checkerboard slices to be thicker.

6. Slice, use in project, and bake following manufacturer's directions.

Clay Dough Recipes

Basic Clay Dough

1 cup all-purpose flour

1 cup water

$\frac{1}{2}$ cup (125 mL) salt

1 teaspoon vegetable oil

$\frac{1}{2}$ teaspoon (2 mL) cream of tartar

Food coloring

1. Mix flour, water, salt, oil, and cream of tartar in a saucepan.
2. Cook over medium heat, mixing the entire time, until mixture holds together.
3. Let clay cool.
4. Knead on a floured surface.
5. Divide dough into smaller balls and add a different color of food coloring to each ball.
6. Knead color into dough.
7. Store each color in a separate airtight container.

Variation:

For intense colors use cake-decorating paste in place of food coloring.

Hint: Dough may be used over and over again and can be stored in the refrigerator for weeks.

Easy No-Cook Dough

This is the best dough to use with very young children who want to do everything themselves!

1 cup all-purpose flour

$\frac{3}{8}$ cup (90 mL) salt

$\frac{3}{8}$ cup (90 mL) hot water

Food coloring

1. Have child combine flour and salt in bowl.
2. Have adult pour in the hot water.
3. Child should stir mixture well.
4. Knead on lightly floured surface for at least 5 minutes.
5. Add a few drops of food coloring and continue to knead.
6. Store dough in airtight containers until needed.
7. Refrigerate up to 1 week

Variation:

For intense colors use cake decorating paste in place of food coloring.

Candy Clay

3 cups powdered sugar

$\frac{1}{4}$ cup (60 mL) corn syrup

$\frac{1}{2}$ teaspoon (2 mL) salt

$\frac{1}{2}$ stick ($\frac{1}{4}$ cup/60 mL) margarine, softened and cut into pieces

1 teaspoon vanilla extract

Paste food coloring, desired colors

Toothpicks

1. Put powdered sugar, corn syrup, salt, softened margarine, and vanilla extract into large bowl.
2. Mix ingredients together until the dough does not feel sticky. You may need to add more powdered sugar to make it less sticky (from $\frac{1}{4}$ to $\frac{1}{3}$ cup/60 to 80 mL) but add it slowly. Stop when dough is no longer sticky.
3. Divide the dough into little balls.
4. Using a separate toothpick for each food color, take a small scoop of paste with the toothpick, and "wipe" it on the dough. Make each ball of dough a different color.

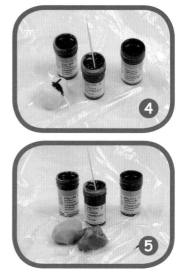

5. Knead the dough with your hands to mix the color.

Note: You can make the color of the clay lighter or darker depending on how much color you add to the clay. Remember: if the clay is too bright a color it will color your teeth when you eat it!

6. Store each color dough in a separate airtight container until you are ready to use it.

7. You can shape and sculpt Candy Clay as you would any modeling dough or put it through a garlic or clay press.

8. Eat immediately—candy clay will not last for days on top of your desserts!

9. Store what you do not use in the refrigerator in airtight containers or plastic bags for up to 3 days.

Square Photo Holder

What You Need:

♥ 4 colors modeling clay

♥ Wire photo holder (can be purchased at your local craft or hobby store or you can make one by bending wire the shape you want)

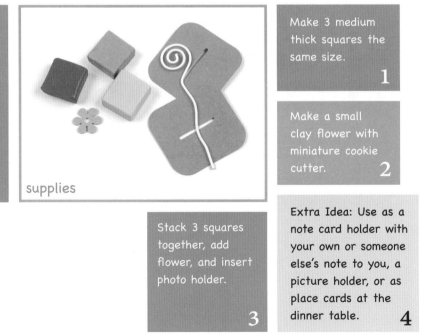

supplies

Make 3 medium thick squares the same size.

1

Make a small clay flower with miniature cookie cutter.

2

Stack 3 squares together, add flower, and insert photo holder.

3

Extra Idea: Use as a note card holder with your own or someone else's note to you, a picture holder, or as place cards at the dinner table.

4

Cupcake

What You Need:

- White, green modeling clay

- 1 additional color of modeling clay

- Plastic photo holder (can be found in cake decorating section of craft store)

- Small cupcake cup

Fill cupcake cup with a ball of white clay. Press down on top so ball fills cup and is slightly rounded. **1**

To make flower petals and leaves, make small balls of clay out of 1 color and green. Flatten ball and pinch one end. Slightly push up edges. **2**

2

Put flower petals and leaves on cupcake. **3**

3

Insert photo holder. **4**

4

Flower Pot

What You Need:

- Brown, green modeling clay
- 2 additional colors of modeling clay
- Burlap — a small strip
- Miniature flower pot and saucer
- Plastic photo holder (these can be purchased in the cake decorating department of your local craft store)

1

Make clay Strip.

1

Place burlap over clay and roll with rolling pin

2

2

Wrap strip around clay pot. Round end, fold over bottom, and trim excess.

3

3

Make thin second clay strip to cover rim of pot. Cut to fit rim. Wrap around rim. Press with your fingers.

4

4

5

Make small flower from clay cutter. Add to pot.

5

Put ball of brown clay into bottom of pot. Fill top of pot with strings of brown clay made from clay press.

6

6

5

Repeat steps 1 - 4 to cover saucer.

7

7

Fill bottom of saucer with green clay.

8

8

Cover clay with "grass" made from clay press.

9

9

Put pot in saucer, put photo holder in pot, add photo or paper to write a name or note on.

10

10

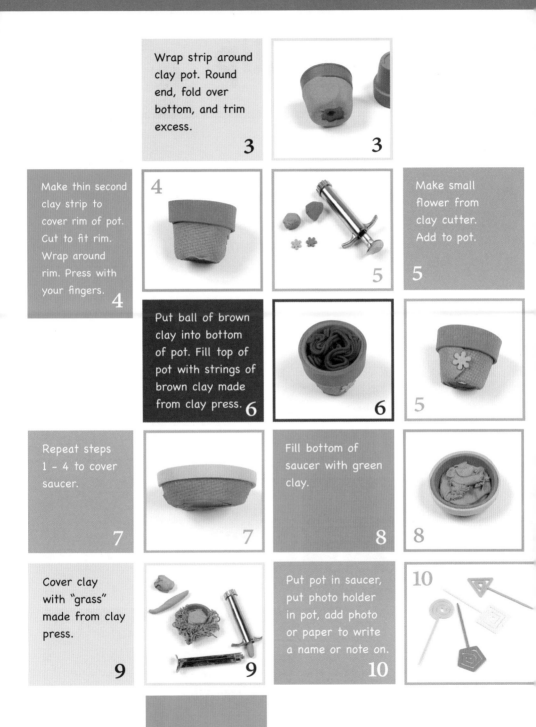

Ladybug Clip

What You Need:

- Red, black modeling clay

- 2 wooden ladybug shapes (can be purchased at your local craft or hobby store or you can cut one yourself from balsa wood)

- Small square block of wood

- Minature wooden clothespin

- Wood glue

Glue small block of wood and clothespin to the back side of one ladybug shape. Let dry.   **1**

Cover 2nd ladybug shape with red modeling clay. Press around edges of shape.   **2**

Add black stripe, dots, and rounded triangular shape for head.   **3**

Glue other half of clothespin to clay-covered shape and let dry. See photo #1.   **4**

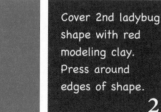

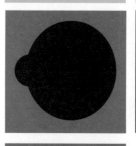

Use as photo or note holder.   **5**

Dump Truck

What You Need:

💜 Black, brown, white modeling clay

💜 2 additional colors of modeling clay

Make Slabs from white and 2 colors of clay. **1**	Cut truck body and cab from slabs. Slightly overlap cab onto body and squish together. **2**
Make Snake from brown clay, place on top edge of truck body, then flatten. **3**	Make a small rectangle window from white clay and place on cab. **4**	Make 2 black balls and squish into circles. Add to body as wheels. **5**
Make 2 smaller white Balls, add to center of black wheels, then squish. **6**	Make 2 tiny black Balls, then add to center of white wheels. **7**	Make D T initials. Make periods with 2 very tiny balls. Flatten onto body. **8**

35

Sailboat

What You Need:

♥ 4 colors modeling clay

Make a Ball and shape into a boat. **1**	Make a Ball and shape into a triangle to make the sails - cut down middle. **2**	Roll a Snake. Place under the bottom of the boat, bring up through triangle, and attach flag at the top as shown. **3**

Airplane

What You Need:

♥ White modeling clay

♥ 4 additional colors of modeling clay

Make Slabs from **1** each of the 4 colors modeling clay. Cut airplane shape from one slab. Cut wing shapes from one slab.	Cut propeller shape from one slab. Cut stars, small triangles, and circle from one slab. **2**

Cut window from white slab. Layer shapes in this order: plane body, wings, stars, triangles, circle, window, propeller. **3**

Taxi

What You Need:

♥ Black, white, yellow modeling clay

Note: Shapes may be made with cookie cutters, knife, and/or scissors.

Make Slab from yellow clay. Make taxi shape. **1**	Make white Slabs and cut into window shapes. Add to taxi. **2**	Make black Snake and add to taxi around windows and down center as door. **3**
		Make 2 black Balls, squish into circles. Add to car shape as wheels. **4**
Make 2 smaller white Balls, add to center of black wheels, then squish. **5**	Make 4 tiny black Balls. Add 2 to center of wheels and 2 to center of doorknobs, then squish. **6**	Following Checkerboard instructions on page 25, make a black-and-white strip and add to taxi as shown. **7**

Flip-flops

What You Need:

♥ Several colors modeling clay

♥ String

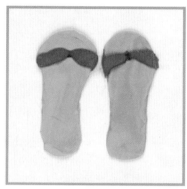

Make 2 small Balls, press flat, shape into flip-flop shape.

1

Make 2 tiny Snakes from clay and add to flip-flops as straps.

2

Lei

Make flowers from several colors of clay using clay cutter. (Make extra flowers for grass skirt.)

1

Make a Snake from 1 color of clay and form a circle.

2

Press flower shapes onto snake circle.

3

Grass Skirt

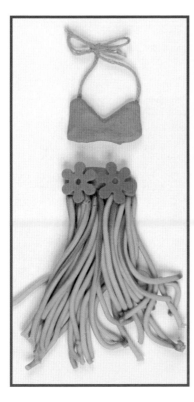

1 Make grass using clay press.

2 Make a small Snake band for skirt and place over top of grass.

3 Place flowers over snake band. Gently press into place.

Bikini Top

1 Make Ball, press, and shape into bikini top.

2 Cut string into 2 pieces. Press into back of top, tie.

39

Castle

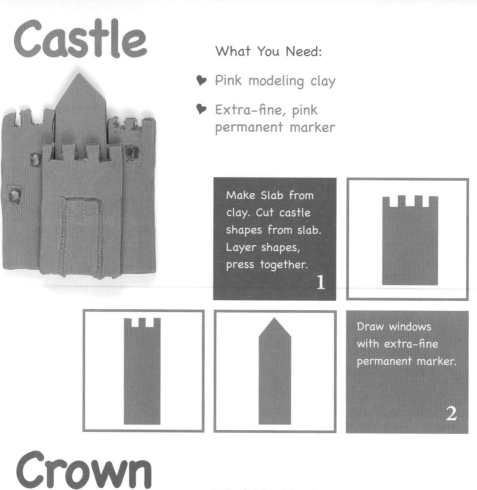

What You Need:

- ♥ Pink modeling clay
- ♥ Extra-fine, pink permanent marker

Make Slab from clay. Cut castle shapes from slab. Layer shapes, press together. **1**

Draw windows with extra-fine permanent marker. **2**

Crown

What You Need:

- ♥ 1 color modeling clay
- ♥ Small rhinestones or different colors of clay balls

Make Slab from clay. Cut crown shape. Add rhinestones or tiny clay balls. **1**

Frog Prince

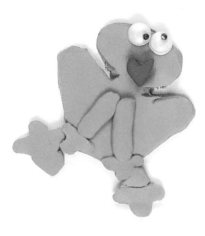

What You Need:

- ♥ Green, red modeling clay
- ♥ Wiggle eyes

Make Slab from green clay. Cut frog shapes, layer, and gently press together. **1**	Add wiggle eyes. Make tiny red oval, shape into elongated heart, and add to frog's face as lips. **2**

Banner

What You Need:

- ♥ Pink, white modeling clay
- ♥ Extra-fine, pink permanent marker
- ♥ 2 rhinestones or different colors of clay balls

Make Slab from white clay. Cut banner shape to any size and shape. **1**	Make small Snake from pink clay, twist into curlicue, and press on top of banner. **2**	Write words on banner or add small paper cut-out sign. **3**	Add rhinestones, or 2 small balls of clay, on either side of word. **4**

Bug

What You Need:

- 💜 Green, orange, pink, yellow modeling clay
- 💜 Extra-fine, black permanent marker
- 💜 Wiggle eyes
- 💜 Toothpick

Make Ball from green clay, then flatten. Or, you can make a Slab, then cut a circle. **1**

Make a smaller Ball from orange clay, flatten, place on body, then press lightly. **2**

Make a small triangle from pink clay and place on head. **3**

Make a star from yellow clay and place on hat. Make a flower from pink clay and place on bug body. **4**

Make a small Snake and cut into two pieces, twist together, cut both ends, place on bug back slightly under body, then press lightly. **5**

Make small Ball, shape into puffy triangle, and place on top of candle. **6**

Make small Balls and decorate bug's body. **7**

Break toothpick into 4 pieces and place under bug body as legs. Add wiggle eyes. Draw mouth. **8**

Caterpillar

What You Need:

- Green, orange, pink, yellow modeling clay
- Extra-fine, black permanent marker
- Wiggle eyes
- Miniature pom-pom, optional

Make Slab from green clay. With small circle cutter cut circles from slab. **1**

Layer circles on top of each other in caterpillar pose. Slightly press circles into each other. **2**

Make small Ball of orange clay, flatten, and shape into triangle. Place on caterpillar's head. Add small yellow ball or pom-pom. **3**

Make small Snake from orange clay. Break off part of it and make curlicue for caterpillar tail. **4**

Divide the rest of the snake into 2 pieces, twist together, cut both ends, place on caterpillar back slightly under one circle, and press slightly. **5**

Add small yellow Ball, shaped into tiny puffy triangle, for flame. **6**

Make small orange balls and place as dots along caterpillar. Add wiggle eyes. Draw mouth. **7**

43

Dragonfly

What You Need:

- ♥ Black, green, orange, purple modeling clay
- ♥ Wiggle eyes

Make small Slab from black clay. Cut two small circles and one medium circle.

1

Make a Slab with orange clay. Cut 3 small circles, forming the end of one into a teardrop shape, as shown.

2

Make four small Slabs from green clay. Cut ovals from slabs.

3

Make 2 small flowers from purple clay using clay press and 2 squiggles by making 2 small Snakes and looping them around on themselves.

4

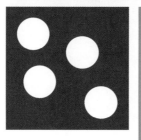

Place wings on tabletop. Alternate orange and black circles, slightly overlapping with the wings to hold them in place. Finish with the teardrop-shaped clay piece. Add small embellishments and wiggle eyes.

5

Turtle

Make Slab from green clay. Cut into a circle, trimming off the bottom as shown to make the turtle body. **1**

Cut a small circle from green clay to make the head. Cut 2 more small circles, pinch into legs, and place slightly under the body. Make a small tail. **2**

Make a small cone from yellow clay and place on the turtle's head for a hat. Add small pom-pom or orange ball to the top of the hat. **3**

Make a small Snake to decorate bottom of shell. **4**

Add rhinestones, or small balls of colored clay, and wiggle eyes. Draw mouth. **5**

Make a small pink Snake and tear into 2 pieces. Twist together, cut both ends, and place on turtle's back, slightly under the large circle. Press slightly to hold. **6**

Add small yellow Ball, shaped into tiny puffy triangle, for flame. **7**

Lizard

What You Need:

- Green, black, orange modeling clay
- Wiggle eyes

Make Snake from orange clay, flatten into lizard body, and round one end as head. **1**

Make 4 small Snakes, flatten, and place slightly under lizard body. **2**

Make 12 small Balls. Place 3 on each leg, then flatten on top of each other to make lizard feet. **3**

Make small green Snakes and decorate lizard tail. **4**

Make small black Balls and decorate lizard body. Add wiggle eyes. **5**

Ladybug

What You Need:

- Black, green, pink modeling clay
- Wiggle eyes

Make 2 Ovals from green clay and 1 Oval from black clay. Flatten all ovals between your hands so they are not so thick. **1**

Put down black oval, place green ovals on top for wings. Make tiny pink Balls and decorate wings. Add wiggle eyes. **2**

Hats

What You Need:

- ♥ A variety of colors of modeling clay

- ♥ Pom-poms, feathers, misc. embellishments, optional

Make 1 Slab each from each color of clay. **1**	Cut out triangle shapes from slabs using scissors or knife. Use cookie cutters to make cutouts. **2**	Roll triangle shape so that the edges overlap in the back. Wet the clay a little with water and press edges together. **3**

Decorate with small cutouts. Add pom-pom, feather, ball of clay, or other embellishment to hat tops. **4**	

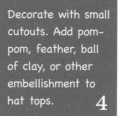

Cake

What You Need:

- ♥ Orange, pink, purple modeling clay
- ♥ Toothpick
- ♥ Cake confetti, optional

> Make a big Ball from pink clay, flatten on top and bottom.
>
> **1**

> Using scissors or fondant cutter cut a trim piece from purple clay, press to bottom of cake.
>
> **2**

> Break a toothpick into 4 equal pieces, insert into cake top.
>
> **3**

> Make 4 very tiny tear drop flames and mold onto toothpick. Sprinkle with confetti.
>
> **4**

Present

What You Need:

- ♥ Pink, purple modeling clay

> Make 1 Slab each from both pink and purple clay. Cut out package shape from purple using scissors or knife.
>
> **1**

> Cut out 4 triangles, and 1 square strip from pink clay. Cut strip and layer pieces to create package.
>
> **2**

Yellow Dog–
Red Dog

What You Need:

- A variety of colors of modeling clay

- Extra-fine, black permanent marker

- Embellishments, optional

1 Make 1 Slab from each color of clay. Cut out dog-face shapes, ear shapes, and small triangles for hats.

2 Attach ears to face and hat to top of head. Make eyes and nose with marker or very small balls of clay. Draw faces.

Yellow Cat–Blue Cat

What You Need:

- A variety of colors of modeling clay

- Extra-fine, black permanent marker

- Fine wire

- Embellishments, optional

1 Make 1 Slab from each color of clay. Cut out cat face shapes, crown, and triangle with scissors or knife.

2 Attach crown and hat to heads. Make eyes, nose, and mouth with marker or very small balls of clay.

3 Cut wire into short lengths, insert into cat's face as whiskers.

49

Party Fish
Princess Fish

What You Need:

- ♥ A variety of colors of modeling clay
- ♥ Extra-fine, black permanent marker
- ♥ Black string
- ♥ Pom-pom, optional

Make 1 Slab from each color of clay. Cut out fat oblong for fish body. Cut out triangles for fish tales. Slice one tail with knife and pinch in second tail. (See photo) **1**

Cut a triangle for hat and cut out crown shape. Turn fish body over, with a small amount of water attach the end of the tail and the two cut ends of string. Press lightly. **2**

Turn fish body right side up, put crown and hat on heads, make eyes, make lips or draw with marker, add pom-pom or small ball to hat. **3**

Faces

What You Need:

- A variety of colors of modeling clay

- Wiggle eyes

- Fine wire, feather, pom-poms, and other embellishments, optional

Make 1 Slab from each color of clay. Cut faces with square cookie cutters, knife, or scissors. **1**

Make hair using a clay press. When attaching hair put a tiny bit of water on the face and put hair on top. Gently press, but do not smash the hair pieces together. **2**

Add wiggle eyes or make eyes from clay. Make lips and tongues. Some mouths are made by using a fine tool like a wood skewer to make mouth impression. **3**

There is no right or wrong way to make these faces. Mix and match colors, mouths, hats, and just have fun! **4**

Easter

Basket

What You Need:

♥ Blue, green, pink, orange, purple, yellow, white modeling clay

Make a large fat Sausage. Hollow out the middle of the sausage about ½ of the way down from one end. **1**

Make 2 Balls and squish into ear shapes. Make grass with garlic press and put in top of hollowed out basket. **2**

Make a little triangle nose, 2 small eyes, and tiny colored eggs. **3**

Make 2 Snakes and twist them together to make the handle. Wet the inside of the basket where the handle will go and press handle ends into basket sides. **4**

Carrot

Make a Sausage. Mold into carrot shape. Add leaves using a garlic press. Put leaves under the carrot and press slightly to hold in place. **1**

Egg

Make an Oval. Flatten bottom on table so egg will stand up. **1**

Make decorations for egg using the clay press and the fondant cutting wheel. Wet egg slightly where decorations will go, put decorations in place, and press lightly to adhere. **2**

Chicken

What You Need:

- ❤ Black, orange, yellow modeling clay

- ❤ Extra-fine, black permanent marker

- ❤ Variety of clay colors for embellishments

- ❤ Feathers

Make a Slab from yellow clay. Cut into 1 large and 1 medium size circles. **1**

Wet top of large circle and place medium circle on top. Make a long, very skinny Snake from black clay. **2**

Take 3 pieces from the snake and make one leg, put the end up under the large circle and lightly press. **3**

Repeat with other leg. Make flower and head band for the chicken's hat and put on top of head. **4**

Make a triangle from orange clay for the beak and mark eyes with marker. Stick feathers into the clay around the top half of the body. **5**

53

Mother's Day

Butterfly

What You Need:

- ♥ Black, red, white modeling clay

> Make a Slab from red modeling clay. Cut out 2 large red hearts, 2 medium white and 1 medium red heart, 2 small red hearts. Cut medium red heart in half. **1**

> Layer hearts to make wings. Body is made from a Snake and a small Ball for the head. The antennas are 2 small Snakes. **2**

Heart Tag

Color me blue without you

What You Need:

- ♥ Blue modeling clay
- ♥ Small blue colored pencil
- ♥ Tag

> Make a small Slab of blue clay, cut out heart. Paste heart and pencil to tag. Write message on tag. **1**

Rose Cupcake

What You Need:

- ♥ Green, red, white modeling clay
- ♥ Red cupcake cup

1 Fill cupcake cup with a ball of white clay large enough to fill cup so that it is slightly over the top.

2 Tear a few pieces of white clay and add to top of ball in cup to look like frosting.

To make rose:

1 Make one very thin Slab of green and 1 of red clay. Using cookie cutter cut 2 ovals of green and 2 ovals of red.

1

3 Cut out 3 tiny hearts from red slab. Make rose, place on top of cupcake with 3 hearts.

2 Place oval horizontally in front of you and roll up the oval so that it is tighter at one end than the other.

2

3 Repeat with other 2 green ovals. Lay the 2nd red oval in front of you on the table, place the rolled oval from step 2 in the middle of this oval and wrap 2nd oval around first.

3

4 Gently pinch the bottom of the rose. Gently roll the edges of the petals back.

5 Roll edges of green leaves back. Put one green leaf on each side of rose. Place rose on cupcake. Add 3 small hearts.

5

Halloween

What You Need:

♥ Black, orange, brown modeling clay

♥ Wiggle eyes

♥ Hand buttons, optional

Make a Ball of orange clay, flatten on the table so that the middle of the ball is still slightly rounded. **1**

From black clay make a triangle for the nose and a tongue. Place on pumpkin. Add wiggle eyes. **2**

Make a small Sausage from brown clay and mold into stem shape. Add button hands if desired. **3**

Boo Banner

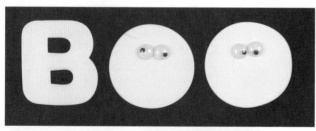

What You Need:

♥ White, black modeling clay

♥ Wiggle eyes

♥ Letter B&O cookie cutters

Make 1 Slab from white clay and 1 Slab from black clay. Using cookie cutter cut letters from white. **1**

Using a knife cut a rectangle from black so that BOO will fit. Add wiggle eyes. **2**

Spider

What You Need:

- ♥ Black, orange modeling clay.
- ♥ Toothpicks
- ♥ Wiggle eyes
- ♥ Pom-pom, optional

Make Slab from black clay. Make small Slabs of orange clay. **1**	From black slab cut out a circle for spider body. Make 6 small Snakes and attach to the back of the body. **2**	Cut a triangle from orange, put on spider, add pom-pom or black ball. Add wiggle eyes. **3**

Cyclops Suckers

What You Need:

- ♥ Black, orange modeling clay.
- ♥ Toothpicks
- ♥ Wiggle eyes
- ♥ Flower cookie cutter

Take a Ball of orange and a Ball of black clay. Marble following Marbling directions on page 22. **1**	Make a Slab from marbled clay, cut out suckers using a cookie cutter. Add toothpicks and wiggle eyes. **2**

Christmas

Christmas Tree

What You Need:

♥ Brown, green, red modeling clay

♥ Star

♥ Heart-shaped cookie cutter

Make a Slab from green clay. Cut a series of tiny hearts from slab. Layer hearts to make tree. (See photo). **1**

Make tiny red Balls to make ornaments for the tree. Make a small brown square and use as tree trunk. Add star on top. **2**

Note: If you do not have brown clay you can mix green and orange clay together and it will make brown.

Wreath

What You Need:

♥ Green, red modeling clay

♥ Heart-shaped cookie cutter

Make a Slab from green clay. Cut a series of tiny hearts from slab. Arrange hearts to look like a wreath. (See photo) **1**

Add small red Balls to look like berries. **2**

Light Garland

What You Need:

- ♥ Black, green, red, white modeling clay
- ♥ Black string

Marble white and green clay together following Marbling directions on page 22. **1**	Repeat with white and red clay. Make marbled clay as well as red, green, white, and black clay into Slabs. **2**	Cut small circles from each of the slabs. Cut black circles in half. Squish black half circles onto colored circles. Lay on top of black string. **3**

Snowman

What You Need:

- ♥ Black, orange, red, white modeling clay

		Make 1 Slab from both white and black clay. Cut 3 circles the same size from white clay. **1**
	Cut a rectangle, a narrow strip, and 4 little squares from black clay. Layer circles to make a snowman. **2**	Add hat and circles. Make 2 Balls for eyes and a little pointed orange nose. Add tiny red Snake to hat to look like a ribbon. **3**

59

Snake Ring

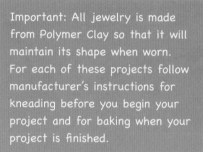

Important: All jewelry is made from Polymer Clay so that it will maintain its shape when worn. For each of these projects follow manufacturer's instructions for kneading before you begin your project and for baking when your project is finished.

What You Need:

♥ Orange Polymer clay

♥ Orange rhinestone, optional

Make a Snake from orange clay. Twist around something that is about the size of your finger. **1**

Press rhinestone into place, then remove, and set aside. Bake. Glue rhinestone in place. **2**

I Love You Bracelet

What You Need:

♥ Pink, red Polymer Clay

♥ Extra-fine, black permanent marker

♥ Black elastic

♥ Toothpick

Make very thick Slabs from pink and red clay. Cut 4 square beads and 1 heart bead from slabs. **1**

Insert toothpick through squares and heart. Twist the toothpick to make the hole large enough. Bake. **2**

Write I and YOU on the square beads. String onto elastic. Give to a friend for her birthday or to mom just because! **3**

Smiley Face Bracelet

What You Need:

- ♥ A variety of colors of Polymer clay
- ♥ Extra-fine, black permanent marker
- ♥ Elastic
- ♥ Toothpick or wood skewer

Make very thick Slabs of clay from each color. Now make very thin Slabs from 2 colors. **1**

From thick slabs cut **2** a variety of shapes using cookie cutters or a knife. Put toothpick through each shape, twist to enlarge hole.

From thin slabs cut 2 circles and letter O – remove center from O. **3**

Draw smiley faces on circles and put a peace sign shape made from a very thin snake in the middle of the O. **4**

Bake beads separately from smiley faces and peace sign. Because beads are so much thicker they will take considerably longer to bake. **5**

Glue smiley faces and peace sign to middle of flowers. String bracelet on elastic cord. **6**

Beads

Beads made from Polymer Clay can be made using any of the techniques talked about in this book. You can marble the clay, twist snakes together, roll it into balls, make squares or triangles, cut shapes with tiny cookie cutters, and you can layer the clay to make dimensional objects. You can even paint the clay or glue glitter onto it when your projects are finished baking. The only thing you must remember to do is to punch a hole somewhere in the bead so that you can string it.

Use your imagination and make enough beads for everyone you know!

Flip-flop Bracelet

What You Need:

- ♥ A variety of colors of Polymer Clay
- ♥ Black elastic
- ♥ Small eyelets
- ♥ Toothpick

Make Balls from a variety of colors of clay. Flatten on 2 sides. Make holes through each ball with toothpick. **1**

Make flip-flops (page 38). Screw eyelets into top of flip-flops. Remove eyelets. **2**

Bake. Glue glitter to flip-flops. Re-insert eyelets, securing with glue. String onto elastic. **3**

Flower Pin

What You Need:

♥ Blue, orange, yellow Polymer Clay

♥ Extra-fine, black permanent marker

♥ Pin back

Make a Slab from the blue clay. Cut 5 large circles and arrange in a circle. **1**	Make 4 orange Balls, flatten, and arrange on top of blue circles. **2**	Make a yellow Ball, flatten, and place in the middle of the flower. Bake. Glue pin back to back of flower. **3**

Bird Pin

What You Need:

♥ Blue, yellow modeling clay

♥ Extra-fine, black permanent marker

♥ Pin Back

Cut 1 large circle and 1 small circle from Slab of blue. Moisten section of large circle where small circle will go. Place small circle and lightly press. **1**	Make 2 ovals for wings, cut a small heart and place it under large circle for tail feathers, make 3 yellow triangles – 2 for feet and 1 for a beak. **2**	Make pin dot with marker for eye. Bake. Glue pin back to back of blue bird. **3**

Clay Index